DISSENT OF THOUGHTS

PRANSHU VATS

Copyright © Pranshu Vats
All Rights Reserved.

This book has been self-published with all reasonable efforts taken to make the material error-free by the author. No part of this book shall be used, reproduced in any manner whatsoever without written permission from the author, except in the case of brief quotations embodied in critical articles and reviews.

The Author of this book is solely responsible and liable for its content including but not limited to the views, representations, descriptions, statements, information, opinions and references ["Content"]. The Content of this book shall not constitute or be construed or deemed to reflect the opinion or expression of the Publisher or Editor. Neither the Publisher nor Editor endorse or approve the Content of this book or guarantee the reliability, accuracy or completeness of the Content published herein and do not make any representations or warranties of any kind, express or implied, including but not limited to the implied warranties of merchantability, fitness for a particular purpose. The Publisher and Editor shall not be liable whatsoever for any errors, omissions, whether such errors or omissions result from negligence, accident, or any other cause or claims for loss or damages of any kind, including without limitation, indirect or consequential loss or damage arising out of use, inability to use, or about the reliability, accuracy or sufficiency of the information contained in this book.

Made with ♥ on the Notion Press Platform
www.notionpress.com

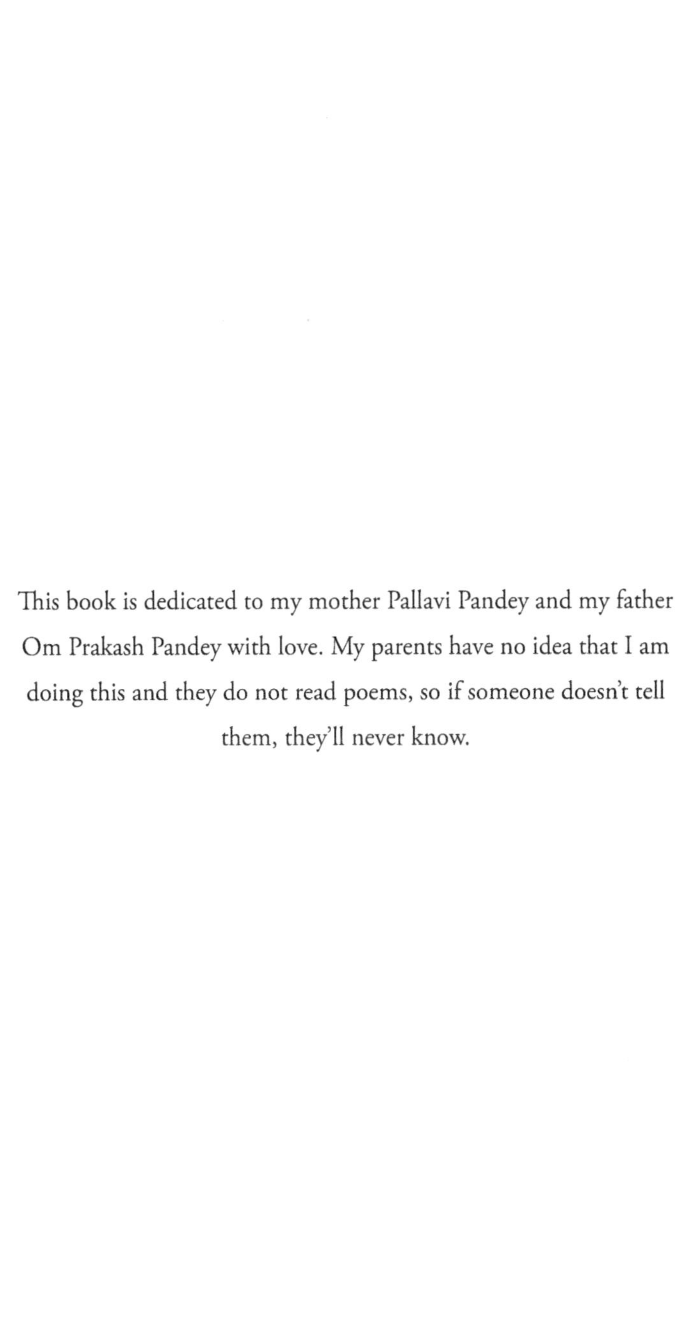

This book is dedicated to my mother Pallavi Pandey and my father Om Prakash Pandey with love. My parents have no idea that I am doing this and they do not read poems, so if someone doesn't tell them, they'll never know.

Contents

Contents

Preface

"Go then, my little Book, and show to all

    That entertain and bid thee welcome shall,

    What thou dost keep close shut up in thy breast;

    And wish what thou dost show them may be blest

    To them for good, may make them choose to be

    Pilgrims better, by far, than thee or me.

    Tell them of Mercy; she is one

    Who early hath her pilgrimage begun.

    Yea, let young damsels learn of her to prize

    The world which is to come, and so be wise;

    For little tripping maids may follow God Along the ways which saintly feet have trod."

    --Adapted from John Bunyan.

Acknowledgements

I wish to express my gratitude to my teacher Mr. Stalin Arnold of Christ University, Bangalore for giving me an idea to write this book and helping me with it.

Thank you everyone who jogged my memory and who contributed to my amazing life.

Prologue

Today I am starting my journey to my success,
I know I am gonna create a lot of mess.
        The effort you put in is more important than the result,
People are always ready to laugh to at your insult.
        If you fight against the society,
You've won the greatest fight,
Then there no hurdle between you and your future bright.
        It's your journey, make it worth,
If you are strong enough,
You can conquer the whole Earth.
        This journey will never end,
You will never be satisfied with your success,
And sometimes it's ok to create a mess.
        -Pranshu Vats

1. She Woke Up Different One Day.....

She woke up different one day,
Bleeding red in sheet
Blenched, she ran to her mother,
With trembling feeble feet.
Mother!, I am hurt, and
Bleeding all over the place,
Please do something, oh mother!
I've read, it brings disgrace
Disgrace is just a lie,
You're pure my child
She cleaned her, held her palms
Looked at her, and then smiled.
Blessed by the goddess,
A boon is bestowed on you,
Now you hold immense power
To hold a life in you
Will I bleed again?
What if someone knew?
They judge us when we bleed,
It's sad but it's true

But you're strong, grow stronger,
With every passing day,
Be the women, fearing no one,
No matter what they say.

• 2 •

2. "SHE"

She can be bright,
She can bring light,
But she doesn't trust her own shadow,
And when the world is only tears and gash,
Her mind leads her to the valley of death,
Not to visit the death itself,
But to become allies,
As to find an escape,
She can be strong,
She can bring a song,
But she fears her own heart,
And when her fortress is a house of treason,
Her warmth longs for the cold of night,
To hold and to twine,
To find comfort in solitude,
To find a friend in loneliness,
She's the star that shines merrily,
That living souls lift their hands to pray to,
But only one with truthful eyes can see her scars,
And name them beauty.

3. You are Mine

Your wounds are mine for healing,
You could fall and scrape your knee,
Your wounds are mine for mending,
For i know it is I, you fell for me.
Your skin is mine for touching,
Your temperature is low; this cold world
Your skin is mine for the warming,
For my grip on you, is beyond absurd.
Your body is mine for the embracing,
When this life drives you crazy,
Your body is mine for holding,
On a sad day no matter how rainy.
Your lips are mine for kissing,
When your soul feels empty,
Your eyes are mine for glancing,
Your tears, I wipe away gently.
Your love is mine for taking,
My love is yours to keep
Your future, ours for the making.
In my arms i will rock you to sleep.
I'll take care of that,
I'll take care of you,

For i do not trust anyone,
That is not me, with you.

4. Suppressed Humanity of a Man

A suppressed humanity lies beneath the skin of every man,
Forced to be strong all the time,
A delicate soul inside the rigid shape of fragile bones but
muscular, his eyes too want to drip in agony.
And brown lips too want to scream,
He too has a heart.
It too aches; he too weeps but fears to make any sound.
He too has dreams to paint her between the silence of midnight,
to fall for his beloved lady, to rest in her love melodies.
His white iris hid crimson pain.
The head is flooded by responsibilities, worries, and myths.
He smiles like an innocent child,
He looks like an old tree holding too many peaceful vibes.

5. "A Filthy Female Creature"

It was a cold,calm night of september, sky hold the white
amicable moon so proud.
The earth welcomed petite,pretty baby girl moon,which was
envied and
embraced warmthly brought heaven;
Yet gloomy, shady feeling
crept over the hearts,it was an invisible cry over smiling fangs a
silent lament disgracing
because it was feminine.
It is an invisible curb holding her down
metaphored as her purity shaded with no certainty.
It is an invisible stigma defining her personality vulnerable to be
called
"A filthy female creature".
There is an invisible tear rolling down her cheeks masked
perfectly behind her smile and named it is her rules.
Slowly making her wholly invisible...

6. The Dance of Destruction

The world is your stage, and you are a performer
Dancing around fire creating thunderstorms all over
Layers of Ash on forehead and a damroo in hand
You shatter the universe ,and all the holy lands
Our egos and distress,crawled in your braided hair
You stand atop that demon of our ignorant affairs
You wear snakes and skulls,as your eternal crown
Tiger skin draped on your body,as a sacred gown
Fuming with energy of the Shiva Tandava dance
The whole world is held hostage to your hypnotic trance
Beat of Damroo giving rhythm to your every step
Crescent moon shines with Ganga seated on your head
All the gods and goddesses watch in fear from the sky
The fiery Rudra with a fire,raging from his third eye
Defeating the darkness and all the evils of corruption
We are honoured to watch your Dance of Destruction.

7. Life of a Plant

(Birth)
At the dead of the night
When the sky was blind
She emerged from the soil with tiny leaves.
(First love - teenage)
Enamoured of the golden Sun
She tried to fly in the sky
Her leaves became wings
But her roots were chains.
(Power of Love)
Despite being chained to the soil
She reached closer to the sun
Moving away from the earth
By growing up every moment.
(Heartbreak)
The Sun ignored her and left
Towards the unknown horizon
Breaking her tender heart
Shattering her dreams.
(Aftermath - Adulthood)
She went restless
And searched for love

Birds and bees used her
Then left her for new ones.
(Self-destruction - middle age)
Devoid of sparkling petals
Devoid of luscious nectar
Carrying the burden of remorse
She fell hard on the ground.
(Last love / Awakening - old age)
She kissed the same soil that once she abhorred
Her warm tears filled the soil
And she merged into the darkness.

8. She and You

She brings you to life.
She becomes your wife.
She wipes your tears.
She sacrifices her years.

You call her names.
You wash her flames.
You bring her down.
You steal her crown.

She builds her mind.
She's kind.
She defines beauty.
She defies cruelty.
You give her scars.
You ruin her stars.
You snatch her rights.
You mock her fights.

She rises up.
She toughens up.
She builds empires.

She inspires.

You kill her might.
You strangle her sight.
You forget her gift.
You create a rift.

She will dance in rain.
She will hide her pain.
She will teach the world
to smile again.

9. Impure

Shhhhh!! Go Inside!! You Are
Impure!!
Hahahahaha!! See That Red Stain
On Her Pants..
Stop This!!
They Bleed to Breed!
You Don't Have Any Right To Laugh
At A Girl Who's On Her Periods!
You Don't Have Any Right To Speak
shit!!
She Handles The Pain Herself, The
Mood Swings, The Irritation And
Much More When She's On Her
Periods..
You Just Laugh And Judge Her
Unaware Of The Pain She's Going
Through.. Remember, You Are Here
Only Because Your Mother Used To
Bleed...

10. Let them Judge!

*Hey, You have that talent
in you and you know it.
But, you don't go for it.
Can I ask you why?
But you wouldn't reply.
Well, the answer is
nothing but the fear.
The fear of being judged
is stopping you from
achieving your dreams.
People out there, judge
you because they are
incapable of doing it.
Someone who really does
something to achieve
their dreams would never
judge because they know
about the hardships
involved in it.
So, never fear about
being judged!
Judging is all they can do*

*while you follow your
heart and live your dream.
Therefore, let them judge
and you achieve.*

11. Wailing Women

*Age seven, happiness hibernated, chocolates tasted bitter in his
laps
terror clutched her skin for what if it was a just a touch perhaps.
Demonic lips tasted dripping innocence, sinful hands above
abdomen, oh how he chiseled layers of lust and she veiled under
tag of women!*

*Age fifteen barrened beauty,
pounding heartbeats sealed under
cover horrifying horns chasing her footprints labelling themselves
as her lover
Sombre sunsets gulped down the stories of scars and casualty, oh
how he held and stained her body
with saliva of sensuality!
Age twenty
Morality measured through length of skirt
wishes weighed down by bangle
Red lipstick, gallant giggles all heinous crimes with weapon of
slut sandal
she catches in arms of her amor hypocrite crowd claims it as sin
oh how the prison of hoax pride pierced her peace with torment
pins!*

*Age thirty three, mornings mourns illusive identity as she swaps
silence with smirk. Three children at home waiting as she drapes
her demolished dignity at work fingers fails to carry the weight of
the wedding ring as she clears the garbage. Oh how they chained
her daring dreams and murdered her hope for the sake of
marriage!!*

*Age forty five, puffed eyes perceives the imagery of white widow
in the mirror, screams of scars, rashes of restlessness it all appears
clearer*

*Plethora of past paints her life story with hues of horror
Oh how she embraced the fatal fate by calling it a
manufacturing error!!*

*Age sixty her last breath celebrates bruises as her body decorates
death bed shroud seized ruptured wounds world offered lilies to
her spinning head*

*Cries of cosmos bid farewell to the brave soul, as she journaled
last diary entry*

*Oh how all nightmares composed lament notes, pain buried as
pieces of poetry!!*

12. *FEMALE*

WHO KNOWS HOW SHE IS?
WHO KNOWS HOW IT WOULD BE LIKE SMILING
OUTSIDE AND EXPERIENCING THE PAIN OF
MENSTRUATION?

WHO KNOWS HOW SHE WORKS WHEN ALL THE
BLOOD IN HER BODY GETS SUCKED OUT DURING
THAT CYCLE?

IT'S HARD TO FEEL HER PAIN, IT'S HARD TO GUESS
HER SUFFERING,
IT'S HARD TO BE LIKE HER FOR A
DAY,
NO ONE CAN ANSWER AS IT'S A MATTER OF
BIOLOGY,
BUT ONE MAY TREAT HER IN THE WAY SHE WANTS
TO BE TREATED, AND EVERY "SHE" DESERVES
RESPECT.

13. She Bleeds

She bleeds for life, She bleeds for the existence
She bleeds, she endures, she heals,
She is the shrine for procreation
Carrying with herself the womb of the universe, Her flesh, her
blood is the foundation of subsistence
Bearer of life, essence of continuation,
She is an embodiment of nourishing invigoration
As pure as the snowflakes, as divine as an angel
Her blood, her body render holy miracles
Nourishes the womb and gives life to it,
By bleeding she breathes life into bits
Not impure, not unclean, not gross, not foul, She is a woman,
most
sacred of all.

14. Women Attained Victory

*From artified enchantments to sculpted pain she broke each and
every chain
When patriarchy barked and judgements were laid from what
she wore to how she swayed from what she spoke to how she
stared
Everything was targeted with bitterest judgements with every
step she took people threw punishment Sometimes with blames
and sometimes with heinous abuses
Caged she was
In an illogical excuse but she never stopped, she treaded her ways
from shacks of patriarchy
Arose few rays
Enlightening the world
With light of confidence She traversed the forbidden
With absolute persistence
Standing tall and firm
Rewriting the history
With ink of progress
Women attained victory.*

15. She is a Woman

She is a woman, the glory of a man, the epitome of beauty,
She rests in his crown.
"Behind every successful man there is a woman", They say,
But she lends him to the forefront,
Guiding his way.
She is a symbol of tranquility,
Gifted with patience, She plays many roles, on the stage of life.
She spills joy with her coming,
With the spark of her laughter,
She is the heartbeat of
her father,
The only beloved daughter.

16. Truth: A Luxury

Truth is a luxury in our country, luxury for those who spend
errands
Luxury for those who know are senile
Truth is indeed a luxury in our country
A collection of narratives Narratives of individual opinion,
opinion that assists them to enjoy the credit
Credit for their dilemmas…
Why is it so costly? Is it worth only some dollars? Is it just the
power? Or is it just a tool used to protect the opinions of
powerful beings?
Indeed truth is a luxury
Which the poor cannot afford, poor, like us, with evident facts
although gifted with a
voiceless strength that doesn't have a complete chance of
resilience.
Perhaps, the truth is made only for the powerful and rich.

17. Marital Rape is still RAPE

She came to your

house

leaving everything behind

She loved you thinking you are kind

She worshipped you assuming God's authority

You used her thinking she's your property

She served you throughout her life

You raped her thinking your wife

Without her consent

You destroyed her sentiments

She was your responsibility

You showed her brutality

She is not a toy

To be twisted anywhere to

enjoy

Respect a woman you dirt

She is the cause of your birth....

18. Annihilation of Dreams

She had those colourful

wings

and was eager for her flight,

yet the sky was too high full of gloomy clouds, ready to engulf her

passion.

She stood scared but

strong.

Her dreams laid scattered in the garden of patriarchy

along with the bushes of violence

and disrespectful thoughts,

that wounded her badly as she picked up her dreams.

With these painful injuries,

and torn out wings, her soul got trapped in despair.

And with this we lost another queen from being born.

19. I Have Heard

The dawn that grew in tender care,
Was often seen gazing at the noon,
Soon they fell in lasting love, and created Eve, who loved the moon.
A love so deep witnessed by seas,
It made the lonesome clouds weep.
Moody moon built the wall of pride,
So, with no hope, Eve often sighed.
With no end to misery of sweet Eve,
Deceitful stars pleaded her to leave.
With Eve gone, night took her place,
And darkened the kingdom with disgrace.

20. Goddess

Touch upon thy souls, the fire that burns within you, O Maiden
are you the flame or the holder,
confused me
Sensing the holy womb within thyself
You create, you annihilate, who are you?
Some call you wretched or hybrid, who cares?
Whatever you are, at sight you see her
But inside shines the eternal feminine flames
Sparks of both lights up this twin
flame
For you're not its guardians, you're the blaze
The inferno that consumes the evil in thee
The warmth that protects melody of life.

21. One with Nature

The darkening sky invigorates me becomes my muse,
My heart sleeps but my soul awakens.
The earthy splendor irritates my dumb heart to wake up
In the nature's glory.
The tingling taste of love is like milky way galaxy so far,
yet seems so near.
The colourful bloom, the splashes of viridian green gives a
tranquility to my melancholic eyes kissing them with madness.
The raindrops touch my skin like a lover smooth and silky
but tearing my flesh with fervent fancy everytime it embraces
me.
The swishing tear drops from the sky,
Like a distant drummer making sinfonietta;
My eardrum bursts with pleasure
my bohemia spirit dancing with rhapsody
My tryst with Nature was
complete
And I became one with
Nature.

22. Uncrowned Queens

Adorable girls, pretty ladies loyal partners and girlfriends in need
Trustworthy wives and humble moms
Experienced grandma and honourable women
Secretly crowned ladies in
millions
Whispering in their prayers for someone loved
Dedicating their life for someone loved
Working day and night for someone loved
Unlike any crowned queens
Squabbling just for another crown

23. She Survives...

Women are not strong, as she is the strength.
She is the cognizance, of us being Sapiens.
The Wheel is indeed divine,
She is the "Wheel of life".
She is so moth'-sist'-ers, and so is she a wife.
If men are to mineral, still she is to soil.
She is verbatim dharma, subtle-elusive-voile.
She rules infinite hearts.
She annihilates countless heads,
She is tormented to kill or die,
She loves instead.
She is humanly human, when humankind dies.
Yes, nothing remains forever,
Yet, she-the wheel-the
soil survives.
She-the wheel-the soil
survives.

24. MAA

For as long as I can remember,
it was your embrace that veiled all my blunder.
When pills failed to decrease the pain, it was your hand caressing
my forehead, worked the best to relieve my stubborn migraine.
My love for coffee may lessen overtime,
but it is still the smell of your 'chai',
forever afresh in my mind.
When as a kid in dreams I got terrified,
it was you I found beside me, making me feel fortified.

Little are these instances, I wonder how far I'd go if I begin to
trace your influences.
Your divine 'anchal'
protected me,
always from every evil
eye,
It is you, Maa, in a poem, I fail to describe.

About The Author

The author of this book is a law student from Christ University, Bangalore who loves to read books and write poems. He was born in Patna, Bihar and was brought up in Ranchi, Jharkhand. He is currently pursuing his BA LLB(hons.) degree and he aspires to become a judge in the future. He also has some publications in esteemed journals, The International Journal of Legal Research and Analysis being one of them. He dedicates this book to his mom and dad who have always supported him in all the situations.

www.ingramcontent.com/pod-product-compliance
Lightning Source LLC
Chambersburg PA
CBHW020517160726
47991CB00007B/2998